# The Jesus Culture:

## Building a Church for All Nations

by
**Rev. James Dean Reeves**

© 2025 Rev. James Dean Reeves

All rights reserved.

Unless otherwise indicated, Scripture quotations are taken from the **Holy Bible, New International Version (NIV)**. Copyright © 1973, 1978, 1984, 2011 by Biblica, Inc.™ Used by permission. All rights reserved worldwide.

No part of this publication may be reproduced, stored in a retrieval system, or transmitted in any form or by any means—electronic, mechanical, photocopying, recording, or otherwise—without the prior written permission of the author, except for brief quotations used in reviews or academic work.

Published by JDR Ministries, *Swindon, UK*

Printed in the United Kingdom

## DEDICATION

To my Ghanaian family —

who welcomed me as one of their own,

taught me to rinse my dishes,

and showed me what love across cultures looks like.

To my church —

a living mosaic of nations,

who daily remind me that heaven is closer than we think.

And above all,

to Jesus —

the One who unites every tribe and tongue

into one family of grace.

## PREFACE

When I first began this journey, I didn't set out to write a book. I set out to understand why so many churches in the UK — especially those in multicultural communities — were struggling to reflect the diversity around them. What began as reflection and research soon became revelation: the Church is called not just to welcome all nations but to *become* a people shaped by one culture — the **Jesus Culture**.

This book was born from lived experience — from washing dishes in a Ghanaian home to feeling invisible at a cultural event, from laughter around shared meals to tears shed over racial pain and misunderstanding. Each story, lesson, and reflection is part of my own transformation as a white British pastor learning what it truly means to build a church for all nations.

I write not as an expert but as a learner — a man shaped by friendship, by failure, and by grace. The pages that follow are not a formula but an invitation: to think deeply, to love widely, and to build faithfully.

My prayer is that this book will stir a vision of the Church that looks a little more like heaven — diverse yet united, truthful yet gracious, beautifully different yet one in Christ.

May we, together, become the mosaic God is creating — one people, one Spirit, one Saviour, one culture: the Jesus Culture.

— *Rev. James Dean Reeves*
Swindon, United Kingdom
2025

# CHAPTER 1 – WHY MULTICULTURAL CHURCHES MATTER

## THE VISION OF HEAVEN

"After this I looked, and there before me was a great multitude that no one could count, from every nation, tribe, people and language, standing before the throne and before the Lamb. They were wearing white robes and were holding palm branches in their hands." (Revelation 7:9)

That is the future God has promised: a worshipping community drawn from every nation on earth, united in Christ. The Church is meant to be a living preview of this heavenly reality.

The question is: how do we live that out now? How do we embody that heavenly vision in our own communities today? How do we become a church shaped not by our own cultural traditions but by one culture — the Jesus Culture?

**THE CURRENT CHALLENGE**

In Britain, the picture is mixed. Whilst churches collectively are in decline, Britain itself has become increasingly multi-ethnic. Yet paradoxically, many predominantly white British churches seem to be declining the fastest.

By contrast, my observations of churches that are thriving reveal a common factor: they are communities made up of multi-ethnic groups, drawing together diverse Christian cultures and practices. At the same time, many non-white British Christians gravitate toward churches of their own ethnic identity — and many of those churches are vibrant and growing.

This leads me to believe strongly that predominantly white British churches located in multi-ethnic societies will thrive if they transform into communities that are ethnically diverse. Ethnically diverse communities embody biblical ethics and values that are essential for Christian mission and discipleship.

## THE FACTS: MULTICULTURAL CHURCHES GROW

Research and lived experience confirm this: multicultural churches are the fastest-growing churches in the UK. They don't just reflect what heaven looks like — they thrive because they embody the gospel of love, grace, and inclusion.

But when we talk about *inclusion*, we must be clear what we mean. Christian inclusion does **not** mean that we simply affirm or accept every belief, lifestyle, or ideology. It means that all people — from every nation, tribe, culture, and background — are *invited* to come to Jesus, to find belonging in His body, and to be transformed by His truth.

Inclusion in the kingdom is not about erasing truth; it's about extending grace that leads to truth. Grace without truth becomes cheap love — a soft tolerance that avoids difficult conversations and leaves people unchanged. Truth without grace becomes harsh legalism — a rigid dogma that wounds people and shuts the door of mercy.

Jesus held both perfectly. John writes that *"The Word became flesh and made His dwelling among us... full of grace and truth."* (John 1:14) And in John 8, when the woman caught in adultery was brought before Him, Jesus refused to condemn her — **grace** — yet He also told her, *"Go now and leave your life of sin."* — **truth**.

That is the pattern for the Church today. A church for all nations is inclusive of all people, but not of all behaviours or ideologies. We open our arms wide in grace, while standing firm on the truth of Scripture. Grace invites everyone to the table; truth shows the way to freedom once they are there.

This is what real gospel inclusion looks like: **a community where every person is welcomed and loved, and where every life is called to transformation in Christ.**

But let's be real. When we gather people from many nations, we also gather many *values, customs,* and *interpretations of Scripture.* And not every interpretation is healthy or true.

Every culture carries both good and bad theology — areas where the gospel shines brightly and areas where our own cultural assumptions distort it. The goal isn't to pretend that all views are equally right, but to be humble enough to **learn from one another under the authority of Scripture**.

For example, in some African contexts I've experienced a strong emphasis on prosperity — a conviction that faith guarantees blessing, success, and healing. At its best, this theology reveals a vibrant faith in a powerful and generous God. Yet pushed to the extreme, it can drift into triumphalism that overlooks suffering and the mystery of God's timing.

On the other hand, in much of English culture, we can be guilty of the opposite: down-playing God's power to heal or provide, becoming overly cautious or even cynical about the miraculous. One theology insists that healing is guaranteed now if we only have enough faith; the other quietly assumes there will be no healing at all and that suffering must simply be endured.

Somewhere in the middle lies the truth — that God is both compassionate and sovereign, able to heal and yet present in our pain when healing does not come.

That's why we need one another. Multicultural churches are not just colourful communities; they are *learning communities*. When we walk together across cultures, we correct one another's excesses, strengthen one another's weaknesses, and discover a fuller picture of the gospel.

The answer is not to make everyone think or act the same. We are not aiming for cultural uniformity but for **spiritual unity** — to become one people of one mind, not my mind or your mind, but the mind of Christ (Philippians 2:5).

It's only in Him that grace and truth, strength and humility, prosperity and perseverance find their right balance.

**MY OWN JOURNEY**

I have already begun the journey of leading the church where I minister toward becoming a church for all nations. This has not been an abstract idea but a lived pursuit, with real challenges and lessons learned. One of the key moments was a project we launched: an "International

Day" that celebrated and recognised the ethnic diversity already present in our community, while signalling a new beginning of our journey towards being a church for all nations.

In the chapters that follow, I will reflect on my experiences, share results from a questionnaire I conducted with non-white British Christians about the barriers they face in predominantly white British churches, and highlight lessons learned through both success and failure. My hope is that these reflections will help other churches as they walk their own path toward becoming a foretaste of Revelation 7:9 — a true church for all nations.

## CHAPTER 2 – BARRIERS TO BELONGING

**LISTENING TO THE VOICES WE OFTEN MISS**

If we are serious about building a church for all nations, we need to listen to the voices that are often unheard — especially those who have felt excluded or overlooked in predominantly white British churches.

To begin this process, I designed a short questionnaire for non-white British Christians. Only a handful of people completed it — seven in total — but that's all who responded within the time I had (ministry life doesn't always wait for perfect research conditions!).

Of those seven, six were non-white British as intended, and somehow one white British person managed to get hold of the survey and fill it in anyway. I still have no idea how that happened — perhaps they were testing the system, or maybe they just really wanted their voice heard! Ironically, their response was the exact opposite of the others: while all six non-white British respondents said they preferred to belong to a church that is multi-ethnic and inclusive of diverse cultures, the one white British participant said they preferred to belong to a church traditional to white British culture and practices.

It made me smile — but it also made a point. In its own unplanned way, that response perfectly illustrated one of the biggest barriers to becoming a church for all nations.

The irony made me smile, but it also spoke volumes. It revealed something subtle yet significant about the landscape of the British church. Many white British Christians — often without realising it — prefer church life within their own familiar culture. But the same can be true for many non-white British Christians who, in turn, choose to gather in churches that reflect their own ethnic identity.

This is one of the reasons we see so many thriving black-majority and ethnically distinct churches across the UK today. It's not simply a story of exclusion; it's a story of *mutual cultural barriers* and *comfort zones* on both sides of the equation. Some white churches have been slow to open up space for different cultural expressions of worship, while some within the black community have found it difficult to engage with British culture or have held onto false assumptions about white British Christians.

My own Ghanaian family, for example, have chosen not to attend a black-majority church because they want to integrate into the broader culture of the society they now live in. They don't agree that black African Christians should separate into their own congregations — yet they fully understand why many do, given the real challenges of belonging and expression within predominantly white British settings.

So while black and ethnically distinct churches are often vibrant and full of life, their existence also reminds us that there is still a deeper journey of reconciliation ahead — one that requires humility, honesty, and love from *both* sides of the cultural divide.

**CULTURAL AND ETHNIC BARRIERS**

The questionnaire revealed several key barriers that non-white British Christians face when seeking to belong in predominantly white British churches. But it also highlighted that misunderstanding often runs in both directions.

- **Lack of cultural understanding.**

Many white British Christians neither understand nor actively engage with the ethnic cultures of others. Without intentional effort, it's easy to default to what feels comfortable, leaving newcomers feeling like guests rather than family.

- **Different worship expressions.**

Black African Christians, for example, are often vibrant and expressive in worship, while many white British congregations tend to be quieter and more reflective. Both are beautiful in their own way, but if one form dominates, others can feel stifled or unseen.

- **Lack of representation.**

Leadership and service roles in many churches remain overwhelmingly white British, which can unintentionally send the message that opportunities for involvement are limited to a certain group.

- **Hospitality gaps.**

In many non-Western cultures, hospitality is central to community life — homes are open, food is shared, and relationships are deep. By contrast, white British culture often keeps home life private. This difference can create invisible barriers to belonging.

- **Missional focus.**

Many non-white British Christians are drawn to churches with a strong emphasis on evangelism and biblical teaching. Churches that have become more liberal in theology or have lost their evangelistic zeal are often less attractive to them.

- **Cultural misconceptions.**

At the same time, some non-white British Christians can carry their own assumptions about certain denominations. For instance, one of the headings in my questionnaire was "A Spirit-Filled Church." That phrase sparked an interesting conversation. A Nigerian family in our church later shared that other Nigerians they knew locally were surprised they attended a Baptist church — because they assumed it wasn't "Spirit-filled."

They were happy to correct that misunderstanding, assuring them that our church is *very much* a Spirit-filled church! We simply express it differently. Our strength is sound teaching and preaching, rooted in Scripture, yet the same Holy Spirit is at work among us, empowering our worship, mission, and daily life.

These kinds of cultural misconceptions and assumptions — on both sides — remind us that building a church for all nations requires more than goodwill. It takes humility, patience, and honest dialogue so that we can learn from one another and celebrate the many ways the Holy Spirit is present across cultures.

**ONE MIND, ONE PEOPLE**

The truth is, every culture has both beauty and brokenness. No culture has it 100% right. This is why Paul urges us in Philippians 2:5: *"In your relationships with one another, have the same mindset as Christ Jesus."*

Building a church for all nations doesn't mean erasing culture — it means learning to honour one another above ourselves (Romans 12:10), while allowing Jesus to challenge every culture. His kingdom culture cuts across all our customs, even those we think are superior.

## GRACE BETWEEN CULTURES

What is needed most in a multicultural church? Grace. Not everyone will understand your background, customs, or ways of doing things. Paul didn't expect Gentiles to become Jewish before following Jesus. Instead, he kept it simple: *"Abstain from food sacrificed to idols, from blood, from the meat of strangled animals and from sexual immorality. You will do well to avoid these things."* (Acts 15:29)

In other words: keep it simple, stay holy, walk in love.

When one culture does something that offends another, the answer isn't simply to "let it go" or pretend it didn't happen. True unity requires both **grace and truth**, held together in **perfect love**. Grace enables us to forgive and approach one another gently; truth calls us to have the honest conversations that bring understanding and change.

And when someone offends us out of ignorance — which will often happen as we learn each other's ways — our first response must still be grace, but grace that is courageous enough to speak truth in love. This is how Jesus dealt with people: He never excused sin or misunderstanding, yet He always met people with compassion and a heart to restore.

If we can learn to respond like that — refusing bitterness, embracing dialogue, and speaking truth wrapped in love — then even our moments of offence can become opportunities for growth and deeper unity in Christ.

**WHAT PEOPLE ARE REALLY LOOKING FOR**

The questionnaire also revealed what non-white British Christians look for when seeking a church community:

- A place where they are **loved, accepted, embraced, and supported**.
- A church that is **Spirit-filled**, where the presence and power of the Holy Spirit are both experienced and valued.
- A fellowship with a **missional outlook** — committed to evangelism, discipleship, and sound biblical teaching.

- A community where there are **opportunities to serve and contribute**.

The truth is, this is what every believer longs for — white or black, British or immigrant. People find true belonging when they are loved unconditionally, embraced in Christ, rooted in truth, filled with the Spirit, and given space to participate in God's mission together.

# CHAPTER 3 – WORSHIP, CULTURE, AND UNITY

## DIFFERENT EXPRESSIONS, SAME SPIRIT

One of the most visible differences between cultures in church life is the way we worship. In many African contexts, worship is loud, expressive, and vibrant. In many white British contexts, worship tends to be quieter, reflective, and reserved. Neither is wrong — but when people from different traditions come together, clashes can occur.

For example, black African Christians often feel stifled when they cannot freely express themselves in predominantly white British churches. On the other hand, some white British Christians may feel uncomfortable with more exuberant styles.

If we want to build a church for all nations, we must learn not only to tolerate but to embrace these diverse forms of worship. Worship teams should reflect the ethnic mix of the congregation, drawing on different musical styles and worship practices so that everyone sees something of their own culture in the shared worship of the church.

## THE JESUS CULTURE: ONE MIND, ONE PEOPLE

This is where Paul's call in Philippians 2 becomes vital: "In your relationships with one another, have the same mindset as Christ Jesus."

The Jesus Culture is not about **uniformity**, but about **unity** — a unity that is *rooted in Christ*, not in any single culture or tradition. Every culture carries both beauty and brokenness. Each brings expressions of truth that reflect God's image, and each holds customs or attitudes that need to be surrendered to His lordship.

We cannot assume our way of doing things is automatically better or more "spiritual." Instead, we are called to humility — to prefer one another's needs above our own, and to honour what is good and godly in each other's culture **so long as it does not contradict Scripture or the values of Christ's kingdom**.

Romans 12:10 says it plainly: "Be devoted to one another in love. Honour one another above yourselves."

But this kind of honour is always *Christ-centred*. It is the Jesus Culture that cuts across all our customs — even the ones we cherish, or think are right, or assume are better than someone else's. Jesus becomes the measure by which we test every cultural expression, keeping what aligns with His truth and surrendering what doesn't.

When it comes to worship, this means being willing to sing a song that isn't in your native style, or to express praise in a way that stretches you — not because it's comfortable, but because it blesses a brother or sister and glorifies the same Lord. True unity in worship isn't about blending cultures perfectly, but about exalting Christ faithfully.

**WORSHIP AS A FORETASTE OF HEAVEN**

Revelation 7:9 reminds us that heaven's worship is a great multitude from every nation, tribe, people, and language, standing before the throne together. That heavenly scene isn't monochrome. It isn't uniform. It is a mosaic of cultures and languages lifted in one united song.

When we worship together across cultures here on earth, we are giving the world a glimpse of heaven. We are also training our own hearts to love what God loves: diversity united in Christ.

## A PRACTICAL VISION

In my own church, we have begun to take steps toward this vision. Our worship group is intentionally mixed, with singers and musicians from different ethnic backgrounds. On International Day, we brought songs from multiple nations together, and the result was not chaos but beauty.

Worship should be a space where the unity of the Spirit is visible. That means sometimes laying down our preferences for the sake of others. It also means giving room for voices, languages, and styles that might otherwise be sidelined.

If we are willing to do this, our worship can become not a battle of cultural tastes but a foretaste of heaven itself.

## CHAPTER 4 – LEADERSHIP AND REPRESENTATION

### THE LEADERSHIP GAP

One of the strongest themes that emerged from my questionnaire with non-white British Christians was the importance of diverse leadership. When people look at a church's leadership team and see only one culture represented, the message is clear: this is not a place where everyone belongs.

While the Baptist Union of Great Britain has begun to address issues of diversity and inclusion, in reality leadership in most Baptist churches remains overwhelmingly white British. If we want to build churches for all nations, this must change.

Churches need to be intentional:

- **Recognising and releasing the gifts and callings of all peoples.** Leadership diversity isn't about recruiting leaders from diverse ethnic backgrounds just to appear inclusive — it's about acknowledging that God has already placed gifts, callings, and anointing within people from every ethnicity and background. Churches must be intentional in identifying, nurturing, and empowering those gifts so that leadership truly reflects the body of Christ in all its richness.

- **Investing in training** that equips people from across cultures to lead.
- **Opening doors** for those who might otherwise be overlooked.

Representation matters — not because it's a token gesture, but because leadership shapes culture. If the front of the church is always white, then no matter how welcoming the words from the pulpit are, the unspoken message is that leadership is not truly shared.

**BELONGING IN THE BODY**

This ties closely to what Paul writes in 1 Corinthians 12: the church is one body with many parts. Each part has value; each part is necessary.

The reality, though, is that some in the body have often felt unseen or undervalued. Many Christians from minority ethnic backgrounds carry the pain of being part of churches where their culture hasn't been fully recognised or valued. Sometimes, they have experienced exclusion or even hurt at the hands of fellow believers.

To those who carry that pain, I want to echo the encouragement from my sermon on the Jesus Culture: **don't give up on the body of Christ.** Don't walk away from church because of broken people. That would be like leaving the gym because there are unfit people there! We don't come to church because the people are perfect. We come because we serve a perfect Saviour.

**THE COURAGE TO STAY AND CONTRIBUTE**

It takes courage to stay in spaces where you haven't always felt included. But when you stay, when you bring your gifts, your voice, your story, and your leadership, you change the culture from within.

And for those in majority culture leadership, the challenge is just as clear: we must not only make room for others but actively invite them in. Leadership is not just about who holds the microphone but who sets the agenda, who shapes the worship, who disciples the next generation.

If our leadership reflects only one culture, we are not reflecting the body of Christ in its fullness. But if our leadership reflects the global family of God, we show the world a foretaste of the kingdom.

## FROM REPRESENTATION TO TRANSFORMATION

Representation is the first step, but the goal is transformation — creating a culture where leadership is naturally shared across cultures, where belonging is not conditional, and where everyone can see themselves in the story God is writing through the church.

When leadership is diverse, the whole church flourishes. Different perspectives enrich decision-making, different styles of discipleship nurture different gifts, and different cultural expressions of faith strengthen the body of Christ.

This is not about political correctness. It's about biblical completeness. A church for all nations must have leaders from all nations — not just in the pews but at the table.

## CHAPTER 5 – HOSPITALITY AND EVERYDAY LIFE

**A LESSON IN ISOLATION**

I never truly understood what it meant to be a foreigner in isolation until I attended a Ghanaian wake with my spiritual father. He and my spiritual mother, both Ghanaian, are people I love dearly. When we arrived, my Ghanaian parents were seated at the top table, as is tradition, while guests came to pay respects. Because I was not family, I had to sit alone among a room full of Ghanaians I had never met.

No one engaged me in conversation. When food was distributed, it was given to their own people, and I was passed by. I felt isolated, alone, even angry. Eventually, I left the building and sat sulking under a tree until my spiritual parents came out.

This was unusual for me — most of my experience of Ghanaian communities has been one of generous hospitality. Yet this painful moment became an invaluable lesson. I realised that what I had felt that day is often what non-white British Christians feel when they walk into predominantly white churches. They can be present in the room and yet invisible, overlooked, or excluded.

It was a wake-up call for me. I began to notice how often people of different ethnicities are ignored in church settings, not out of malice but because of unconscious "tribal" behaviour — people gravitating to those they already know or feel comfortable with. But for the newcomer, the outsider, or the refugee, this can be crushing.

## THE TRAP OF TRIBALISM

What I began to notice in myself and others was something I can only describe as **tribalism** — the subtle, instinctive tendency to gather with people who look like us, think like us, sound like us, or share our background.

This isn't always malicious. In fact, it's often subconscious. We are all drawn to familiarity because familiarity feels safe. Psychologists call this the "homophily effect" — the human preference for similarity. From an evolutionary point of view, it's rooted in fear and survival: in early human history, belonging to a tribe meant protection, identity, and security. Being outside the tribe often meant danger.

Though we now live in a globalised world, those old instincts still operate in modern ways. In church life, it looks like sticking with our usual friendship circles, sitting in the same spots, and talking mostly with people who share our accent, humour, or history. It feels natural — but it can quietly undermine the unity of the Spirit.

Tribalism tells us: *Stay with your own.*
The gospel tells us: *Break the wall and make one new humanity.* (Ephesians 2:14–16)

In Christ, our primary identity is no longer ethnic, cultural, or national — it's spiritual. Paul said, *"There is neither Jew nor Gentile, slave nor free, male nor female, for you are all one in Christ Jesus."* (Galatians 3:28) That doesn't mean our ethnic or cultural differences disappear; it means they are redeemed and redefined under a higher allegiance — the kingdom of God.

But tribalism is persistent. It resists integration because it's comfortable. It's easier to stay among people who understand our jokes, our food, our language, and our worldview. Yet, as long as comfort defines our community, we will never fully become the church of Revelation 7:9 — the mosaic of heaven.

**RECOGNISING TRIBAL FEAR**

Underneath tribalism is fear — fear of rejection, fear of being misunderstood, fear of losing what feels familiar. Sometimes, this fear disguises itself as preference or practicality: *"I just get on better with my own kind."* But the gospel calls us to love beyond fear. *"Perfect love drives out fear."* (1 John 4:18)

We have to name tribalism for what it is: a form of self-protection that keeps others at a distance. The cross dismantles that. Jesus did not die for one tribe — He died to make one family.

**MOVING FROM TRIBE TO TABLE**

Overcoming tribalism begins with small, deliberate choices:

- Sitting next to someone you wouldn't normally sit with.
- Inviting a person from another background into your home.
- Listening longer and speaking less.
- Learning another's story without trying to correct or compare it.

The table of Christ is the antidote to tribalism. Around His table, there are no insiders or outsiders — just sinners saved by grace, brothers and sisters learning to love as He loves.

If we can move from tribe to table, from safety to sincerity, the church will begin to look like heaven — not a cluster of comfortable groups, but a community of courageous grace.

That experience at the Ghanaian wake was a turning point for me. It was as if a light had been switched on. I suddenly saw how easily tribalism can creep into our church life — not through malice, but through habit and comfort. I realised that if I didn't choose to act differently, I would keep drifting toward what felt familiar and miss the beauty of God's diverse family.

**CHOOSING TO ENGAGE**

From that experience, I made a conscious decision to engage differently. Since then, I have intentionally welcomed and invested time in people who are different from me in culture, ethnicity, or background. I encourage my church members to do the same — to confront their own biases, to resist the pull of tribal comfort, and to step into the beautiful discomfort of diversity.

As I have done this, something remarkable has happened: my sense of belonging has grown, not shrunk. I now count Ghanaians, Nigerians, and Nepalese among my closest spiritual family. They have embraced me as one of their own, and I have embraced their Christ-centred cultures. In many ways, I feel more at home with them than within my own white British culture.

**WASHING THE DISHES (AND RINSING THEM!)**

Another lesson came in a far more ordinary moment: washing up dishes in my Ghanaian home. As a white Brit, I washed dishes the way I had always done — with soapy water, then straight onto the draining board, without rinsing.

My Ghanaian father was horrified. "Do you rinse the soap off your body when you bathe?" he asked.
"Yes," I replied.
"Then why don't you rinse the soap off the dishes? I don't want to eat soap!"

That day I learned not only to rinse my dishes but also that what we think of as "normal" is simply cultural habit. Since then, I have encouraged other white British people to rinse too — partly in humour, but partly in recognition that even small cultural practices can create barriers to fellowship and hospitality.

**LEARNING THE LANGUAGE OF LOVE**

Language is another barrier we must be willing to cross. Many white British people can be arrogant when it comes to English language, expecting the whole world to adapt, while making little effort to learn other languages.

I learned this lesson when conducting a funeral for my Nigerian auntie. She insisted I pronounce Nigerian names correctly, even sending me voice notes to practice. It was hard work, but it mattered. To mispronounce those names would have been an act of disrespect.

Because of my Ghanaian parents, I've also learned their Fante dialect, enough to converse well. When Ghanaians hear me speak in their own tongue, they light up. They embrace me as one of their own. It builds bridges quickly, because making the effort to speak another's language is an act of love.

They often used to joke with me — and even with my Ghanaian parents — about finding me a Ghanaian wife and taking me to Ghana for a proper naming ceremony! At the time, I laughed it off as friendly banter, never imagining how prophetic those jokes might turn out to be.

Since then, I've actually travelled to Ghana with my Ghanaian mum, where I was officially given a Ghanaian name: **Kwame Nyamekye Dadzie**.

- *Kwame* — meaning I was born on a Saturday.

- *Nyamekye* — meaning "God's gift."
- *Dadzie* — my Ghanaian mother's maiden name.

It was a profound and joyful experience — one that deepened my sense of connection with the culture that has shaped so much of my faith journey. And, in a beautiful twist of divine irony, I am now preparing to marry a Ghanaian woman.

When I first wrote this reflection, that was just a humorous thought — now it's my reality. God clearly has a way of writing stories that weave together our ministry, our heritage, and our heart in ways we never expect.

Even so, I've learned that belonging doesn't always come from the big, dramatic gestures. Sometimes it's as simple as learning to pronounce someone's name correctly, or greeting them in their own language. Small acts of honour build bridges of belonging — the kind of bridges the gospel calls us to build every day.

**SHARING IN PAIN AND TRAUMA**

Not all lessons are humorous. During the height of the Black Lives Matter movement following George Floyd's death, I watched my Ghanaian parents grieve deeply. As a white man, I initially struggled with the movement. It made me feel guilty for crimes I hadn't committed, and I worried it was creating more division. But I realised it wasn't about me.

This was about the lived pain of my black brothers and sisters. My role was to listen, to weep with them, to walk with them. That experience taught me to see racism and inequality not as abstract issues but as wounds carried by people I love. It also gave me courage to challenge unconscious bias and discrimination when I see it.

## COMMUNICATION AND CONFRONTATION IN THE FAMILY OF GOD

These lessons connect closely to what Jesus teaches about relationships in the family of God. In Matthew 18:15 He says: *"If your brother or sister sins against you, go and point out their fault, just between the two of you."*

In a multicultural church, misunderstandings are inevitable. Families are messy. We will offend and be offended. The question is: what do we do when that happens?

The Jesus Culture says: don't gossip, don't stew, don't leave. Talk it out. Forgive as Christ forgave you. Show the same grace you've been shown.

When I think back to the Ghanaian wake, I could have walked away bitter. Instead, I let it shape me. When I think of the dishwashing lesson, I could have dismissed it. Instead, I let it change me. When I think of Black Lives Matter, I could have hardened my heart. Instead, I opened my ears.

This is what communication, confrontation, and grace look like in the family of God.

## HOSPITALITY AS THE JESUS CULTURE

Hospitality is not just about food or open homes. It is about creating space for others to belong, even when it costs us. For white British churches, this means making intentional room for different cultures, learning to embrace new ways of doing life together, and resisting the temptation to retreat into what is comfortable.

When we do this, our everyday lives — from the way we wash dishes to the way we worship — become testimonies to the gospel. And our churches become not just gatherings of individuals, but true families where people from every background can say, "I belong here."

## CHAPTER 6 – LIVING THE MOSAIC

### INTERNATIONAL DAY: A STEP FORWARD

On Sunday 14th January 2024, our church hosted its first-ever **International Day**. The aim was to promote Christ-centred unity and diversity among ethnic cultures, raise awareness of unconscious biases, educate one another about our differences, and celebrate the richness already present in our congregation.

The planning team itself was diverse, representing the ethnicities within our community. Together we designed the morning service, an international bring-and-share lunch, and cultural presentations in the afternoon. From start to finish, the day reflected the mosaic of people God had brought together in our church.

I had long carried a vision of our church building displaying the national flags of the countries represented in our fellowship. Leading up to the event, each nationality sponsored their flag to be hung permanently in the sanctuary. On International Day, five flags were launched — Britain, Ghana, Nigeria, South Africa, and Nepal.

For some, this was deeply moving. One Nigerian sister told me that whenever she sees her national flag in her workplace or church, she feels a sense of belonging and acceptance. The flags became more than decoration. They were symbols of our unity in Christ, a visual declaration that this church was her home too.

**A TASTE OF THE NATIONS**

The lunch was a feast of cultures. Each table was organised by nationality, offering food from each heritage. People did not simply stay with their own dishes — they explored, tasted, and enjoyed one another's food. It was an education of the senses, a breaking down of barriers through something as simple as eating together.

Our worship team reflected the same vision, blending songs and styles from different ethnic Christian traditions. After lunch, members of each nationality gave presentations on their country's history, Christianity, and worship culture.

Yet not everything was easy. I was disappointed that many of our white British members left soon after the lunch, not staying for the afternoon. Perhaps this reflects cultural differences in time sensitivity — white British culture tends to be more rigid with schedules, while many other cultures are more flexible. For future International Days, we may need to adapt — either condensing the event or spreading it across two Sundays.

Still, the day was powerful. It was a glimpse of what church can be when people commit to living as one body in Christ without erasing their differences.

**THE MOSAIC OF HEAVEN**

This connects to a powerful biblical image: the mosaic of heaven. Imagine a vast artwork, each piece different in shape, colour, and texture. Alone, each fragment is incomplete. Together, they form a masterpiece. That is what the church is called to be.

In Revelation 7:9 we see the finished picture: people from every nation, tribe, people, and language worshipping before the throne. Our churches are called to be previews of that day — mosaics in progress, where differences don't divide us but unite us in Christ.

International Day was not just an event; it was a symbol of this deeper calling. It showed us that diversity is not something to celebrate once a year but a reality to embody every week. True gospel unity is not tokenism but transformation. It is not a one-off multicultural service, but an ongoing culture of hospitality, humility, and shared life.

**MOVING BEYOND TOKEN DIVERSITY**

We must be careful here. Hosting an international event cannot be our way of "proving" that we are inclusive. A church for all nations is not built by flags on the wall or food on the table, but by the daily practice of welcoming, listening, honouring, and serving across cultures. International events should serve as reminders and catalysts, not replacements, for genuine inclusion.

As I reflected on the day, I knew it could not be the end. It had to be the beginning of a deeper journey. Our annual International Day is now a fixture, but the real work is what happens every Sunday, every small group, every shared meal, and every leadership decision.

The Jesus Culture calls us to move beyond celebration to embodiment. To live as one people shaped not by my culture, or your culture, but by His.

# CONCLUSION – ONE CULTURE: THE JESUS CULTURE

## THE JOURNEY SO FAR

This book has not aimed to provide all the answers, frameworks, or formulas for building a church for all nations. Instead, it has sought to tell a story — one of discovery, humility, and hope.

It is the story of a local church beginning a journey toward becoming a true reflection of the kingdom of God — a community where people from every nation can belong, worship, and serve together as one body in Christ. It is also my personal story: a white British minister learning through friendship, through mistakes, through cross-cultural experiences, and through the grace of brothers and sisters who have expanded my understanding of God's family.

We have looked at real barriers to belonging — from unconscious bias and cultural misunderstanding to differences in worship, leadership, and hospitality. We have seen that transformation doesn't begin with strategies or programmes, but with hearts that are willing to listen and change.

**THE VISION THAT UNITES US**

At the heart of it all is the vision of **Revelation 7:9**: "A great multitude that no one could count, from every nation, tribe, people and language, standing before the throne and before the Lamb."

That's the destination — the family reunion to which all history is heading. The Church on earth is meant to be a preview of that reality: a mosaic of heaven, a living demonstration of God's reconciling power in Christ.

This is what I call **the Jesus Culture** — one body, one people, shaped not by the customs of our birth but by the character of our Saviour.

Ephesians 4:3–6 puts it this way: "Make every effort to keep the unity of the Spirit through the bond of peace. There is one body and one Spirit, just as you were called to one hope when you were called; one Lord, one faith, one baptism; one God and Father of all, who is over all and through all and in all."

The Jesus Culture is our common ground. It calls us to love across divides, to listen across differences, and to lead with humility and grace.

**A CALL TO EMBODY, NOT JUST CELEBRATE**

Let's not settle for token diversity. Let's press on for gospel unity — the kind that looks like Jesus and points the world to Him.

International Days, multicultural services, and moments of celebration are good beginnings, but they must lead us into something deeper. Real unity is lived in the everyday — in homes opened, friendships formed, and leadership shared. It's seen when we learn one another's languages, when we worship in one another's styles, when we bear one another's burdens, and when we forgive one another's offences.

As the Apostle Paul wrote, we are "no longer foreigners and strangers, but fellow citizens with God's people and members of his household" (Ephesians 2:19).

**A CHURCH FOR ALL NATIONS**

The church of the future — and the church that will thrive — is the one that embraces this vision fully: a **church for all nations** that embodies the Jesus Culture. A people who know that diversity is not a threat but a gift, not a challenge to manage but a glory to reveal.

The world around us is searching for belonging, for authenticity, for unity that is more than words. The Church has the answer — not because we are perfect, but because we have a perfect Saviour who is building His Church from every tribe and tongue.

**A MOMENT TO REFLECT AND RESPOND**

As you finish this book, take a moment to ask:

- Where might the Holy Spirit be calling me to change?
- Where have I held onto cultural pride, fear, or comfort?
- Who is God calling me to welcome, to listen to, or to empower?

- How can my church embody the Jesus Culture more fully — in worship, leadership, and community life?

This is not a quick journey. It's a lifelong calling. But it is the call of Christ Himself — to love as He loves, to serve as He serves, and to live as one family redeemed by His grace.

So let's commit ourselves — not just to **celebrate** diversity, but to **embody** it. Let's build churches where people from every background can walk through the doors and say: **"I belong here. Because Jesus is here."**

## ABOUT THE AUTHOR

**Rev. James Dean Reeves** is a British Baptist minister passionate about seeing the Church reflect the heart of Jesus in a multicultural world. He serves in Swindon, leading a congregation on a journey toward becoming a truly multi-ethnic, Christ-centred community.

James is also the pioneer of the *YAC Shack* — a youth evangelism and community outreach initiative in Pembroke Gardens, Moredon — focused on bridging the gap between evangelism and the gathered church in a post-Christendom society.

Deeply committed to cross-cultural ministry, James draws on his experiences within diverse communities, especially the Ghanaian family who helped shape his understanding of Christian fellowship across cultures. He believes that the future of the Church lies in unity without uniformity — in becoming one people under the rule of Christ.

He lives in Swindon and is soon to marry a Ghanaian woman — a living testimony to the very vision he preaches: that the love of Jesus truly transcends culture, colour, and custom.

Printed in Dunstable, United Kingdom